KU-687-107

STITCH, CLOTH, PAPER & PAINT

MIXED MEDIA IDEAS & INSPIRATION

Angie Hughes

SEARCH PRESS

First published in paperback in Great Britain 2011

Search Press Limited
Wellwood, North Farm Road,
Tunbridge Wells, Kent TN2 3DR

First published in hardback in Great Britain 2008

Text copyright © Angie Hughes 2008

Photographs by Roddy Paine Photographic Studios,
except for pages 7, 14, 15, 17, 36, 37, 38, 58, 59, 60, 74,
75, 76, 92 and 93; by Debbie Patterson at Search Press studios.
Photographs and design copyright
© Search Press Ltd 2008

All rights reserved. No part of this book, text, photographs
or illustrations may be reproduced or transmitted in any form
or by any means by print, photoprint, microfilm, microfiche,
photocopier, internet or in any way known or as yet unknown,
or stored in a retrieval system, without written permission
obtained beforehand from Search Press.

ISBN: 978-1-84448-733-2

The Publishers and author can accept no responsibility for
any consequences arising from the information, advice or
instructions given in this publication.

Readers are permitted to reproduce any of the items/patterns
in this book for their personal use, or for the purposes of
selling for charity, free of charge and without the prior
permission of the Publishers. Any use of the items/patterns
for commercial purposes is not permitted without the prior
permission of the Publishers.

Publisher's note
All the step-by-step photographs in this book feature
the author, Angie Hughes, demonstrating mixed media
craftwork. No models have been used.

Printed in Malaysia

STOCKPORT LIBRARIES	
C2001807326	
Bertrams	29/06/2011
746.4	HUG
CH	£12.99

Acknowledgements
Thanks to Edd the editor for peering
over my shoulder and asking all the
pertinent questions, Ann Davies for
her knowledge and experience and all
of the Ledbury Artplace community
for inspiration.

Withdrawn from Stock

STITCH, CLOTH,
PAPER & PAINT

MIXED MEDIA IDEAS & INSPIRATION

STOCKPORT LIBRARIES

C2000 00180 7326

To Jeanette, who taught me
how to 'really see'.

Contents

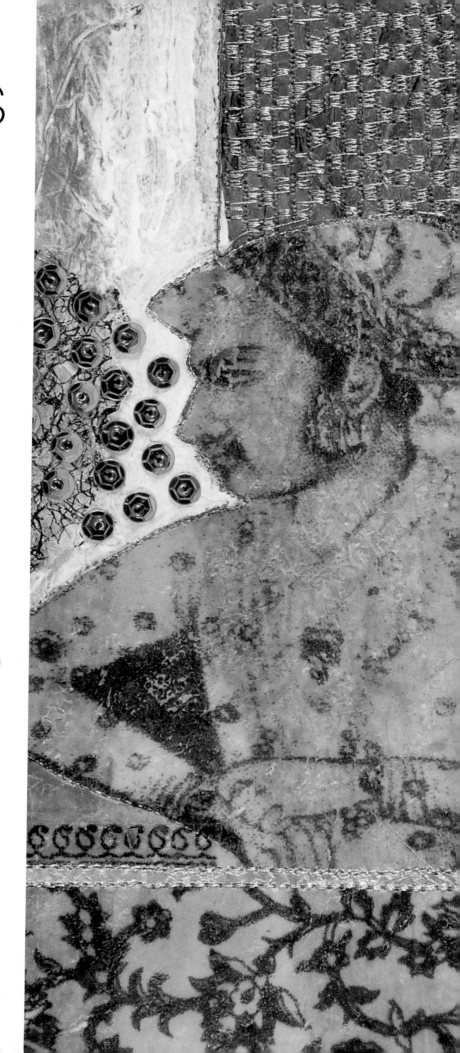

Introduction

I imagine that you might be wondering what mixed media or multi-media art actually is. Think carefully about some of the things you have made in the past: if you have made a Christmas card from fabric, paper, glitter and stitch, you have already used a mixed media technique. In dictionaries, it is described as 'a technique involving the use of two or more artistic media, such as ink and pastel, or painting and collage, that are combined in a single composition'. Of course, any of us interested in textiles would also include thread and stitch.

I began to get interested in mixed media techniques after visiting the Picasso Museum in Paris, where I saw the mix of fabric, paper, bits of wood, rusty nails and old bits of string combined with gesso and pencil drawing that Picasso used in his work. As soon as I got back home, I rushed off to get some gesso and I attempted to echo some of his works. As I learned more, I discovered other artists who triggered my imagination such as Ben Nicholson (who prompted a trip to St Ives), and Turner (you can actually see his brush strokes in the paint). I also came across Rauschenberg, who uses a vast array of materials in his work, including found objects such as old bits of clocks, plastic bags and photographs. My current favourite is Teesha Moore, who mixes media like a maniac and is thoroughly inspirational.

As an embroiderer, I was worried that using heavy paint over fabric and stitch would spoil the nature of the soft surface. In a way, of course, it does: paint hardens fabric; but the intriguing thing is that it can enhance the texture of the surface in a different way. When paint is added to a piece of calico, for example, certain shadows appear when it is dry that you would not necessarily notice in a soft fabric. If you then run some thinned-down acrylic over the surface, the pigment will fall into all of the nooks and crannies, accentuating the shadows.

This book has been designed to help you with the basic mixed media techniques, and it then offers some projects for you to try. I would encourage you to push the boundaries while you are experimenting and to add a favourite technique or material of your own to the mix. There is no right or wrong way of working with mixed media, but I hope that this book helps you to discover your own way.

Indian Book Shrine

Materials

The basic materials for mixed media are very important, so try to collect as many different textural fabrics as you can. It does not have to cost lots of money – in fact, you can usuaully find lace and netting in charity shops.

Strong colours on fabrics will show through one layer of paint, so if you have strong red lace, for example, but your project needs to be pastel blues and greens, you will need to cover the lace in several coats of gesso (see page 16). You risk losing texture with every layer of gesso you paint over the surface, so I use neutral colours to save on the amount of gesso that I need to cover the surface.

Tip
I tend to use natural fabrics to help the paint to be absorbed into the surface – nylon can repel a waterbased paint.

Base fabrics

These fabrics are the ones used to make the basic shape of your pieces, and they are rugged and sturdy. This allows you to decorate your pieces without worrying about them falling apart!

Mediumweight cotton curtain interlining is available from good curtain making suppliers, but you could use pelmet interfacing. I treat the interlining with a PVA solution to get a stitchable, leathery sort of surface.

Mediumweight calico or **plain cotton** can easily be stretched around a canvas after texture, embroidery and embellishments have been added, so both are great base fabrics.

Firm iron-on interfacing is used to stabilise the base fabric.

Stabilizer is a firm manmade surface used, among other things, for stiffening cap brims. When I do not have time to stiffen up some interlining, I use this as a firm backing for my embroideries. It is a good alternative if you can not find interlining.

Decorative fabrics

These are more delicate fabrics that are more suited to decoration than structure, and they give a fantastic variety of texture and interest to your pieces.

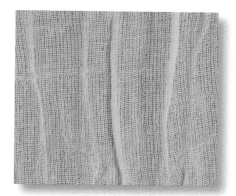

Cheesecloth has deep textural wrinkles that suggest landscape ridges.

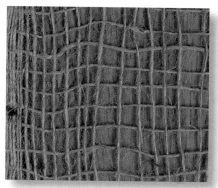

Scrim, **air cloth**, and **plasterers' scrim** are all very open-weave cotton fabrics. You can pull holes and threads about to give a lovely texture for the paint to 'fall' into.

Broderie anglaise is a premade type of lacy edge. It is useful for edging or framing an area of work because of its regular pattern.

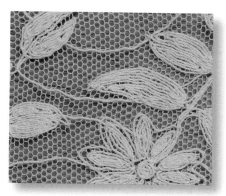

Cotton lace is made from natural fibre as the paint sticks much better. I prefer natural fibres like cotton, but I have met students who have had success with nylon lace and tulle netting.

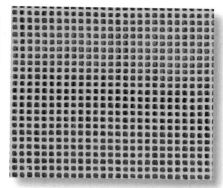

Needlepoint canvas can be stitched and have string knotted into it before you paint. Rug canvas is a good alternative.

Soft linen has a very subtle surface but rougher types look gorgeous when painted.

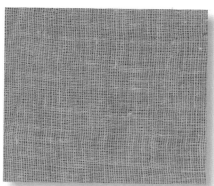

Muslin is not such an open weave as scrim, but it still has a good texture.

Hessian is a natural fabric that is sometimes used as sacking. It has a coarse surface that looks good without any additions.

9

Paper and card

Paper and card are integral parts of the projects in this book. You can scrunch them up for texture and interest, or cut out specific shapes with scissors or punches. They can also be used to make flat texture on which to mount embellishments. Heavier card is utilised to add space between layers in some of the projects later in this book.

Tissue paper I always use recycled dressmakers' tissue as it is thin and crinkles beautifully, but you might like to try acid-free tissue, which can be bought from any art shop.

Paper doilies Get these from your local supermarket: they are available with wonderful designs and can be glued down for a low relief pattern.

Kitchen paper Get hold of a good-quality quilted kitchen paper with a pattern. These make interesting surfaces when wet and they also lift off paint in great patterns when dry.

Plain or **textured thin card** This can be used for all sorts of purposes, from being sewn on to the pre-painted surface in squares to being used as a mount for embellishments after painting. Any old thin cardboard boxes are useful for this kind of thing.

Textured wallpaper A collograph artist alerted me to textured wallpapers. You can get free samples from DIY stores, although you may need to wear a false nose and moustache if you go to the same one too often! (If you are not into dressing up, send a friend.)

Millboard or **mountboard** These stiff cardboards are good for little areas of texture when cut into small pieces. They are also good for mounting and spacing.

Foamcore board This is very handy for mounting and spacing, and is available in art shops. It is used by modelmakers and you can get different thicknesses.

White printer paper This can be decorated with acrylic paints and, once dry, craft punches are used to make embellishments from it. Make sure you use a good-quality weight, such as 100gsm (80lb).

T-shirt transfer paper This is used in the Indian Artefact project (see pages 60–73). Not only can it be used in your inkjet printer so that images can be layered on to fabrics or paper, but it also melts beautifully into the surface of painted tissue paper when ironed on. It can also be stitched over.

Handmade paper All sorts of interesting handmade papers with inclusions like flowers or sequins are available. You will need to experiment with these to see what looks best when you paint over them.

Various types of paper and card.

Threads and sewing equipment

For the projects in this book you will need a **sewing machine**. If you want to buy a machine, you need to look out for one that does a straight stitch and a zig zag stitch. Ideally, you should be able to drop the feed dogs, as this makes some of the techniques a great deal easier.

I prefer a machine that has a separate bobbin case as I use tensioning techniques which involve changing the thread tension in the bobbin. You can do this by turning the grub screw on the bobbin case clockwise to increase the tension (to tighten the thread) or anticlockwise to decrease the tension (and loosen the thread). Do not be discouraged if you have a drop-in bobbin machine which can not be altered: during my workshops, students have achieved the same results with drop-in bobbin machines by simply tightening or loosening the top thread tension.

Ask your sewing machine engineer if they can get you a free machine embroidery foot for your machine. These are very useful for stitching freely without a ring on firm fabric. The foot moves up and down with the needle ensuring all of the tensions are correct while you stitch.

You will also need a few different types of thread. **White cotton** or **poly-cotton thread** is used for most of the basic stitching. I use white threads so that I do not have to paint over too much with gesso to cover up colours.

Ensure you have different thicknesses of **string** for machine and hand couching, while **heavy cords** such as piping or blind cords are very useful. Both heavy cord and string can be couched on to the surface with a zig zag stitch, or by hand if you are a hand stitcher. **Perlé threads** are a bit thicker than normal thread so they show up when painted over. They are mostly used for hand embroidery but can be used on the bobbin or couched down with a zig zag stitch. They look especially nice when stitched into French knots. **Machine-** and **hand-embroidery thread** are useful for embellishing your work. **Metallic threads** are tricky to use as they are a made up of metal, twisted round a thread core, that can shred when stitching. Spend a bit of money on these to get a good-quality thread, as they will run much more smoothly through the machine.

Basic sewing equipment, including **needles, beading needles** and **pins**, are needed for areas that can not be reached by the sewing machine.

My sewing machine.

Opposite:
Some of the threads used in this book.

12

Paints

Acrylic paints Good-quality acrylic paint will help you to get good-quality results. Some cheaper acrylics can be opaque, and since being able to see one colour through another gives the best effects, transparency is important.

I also use **metallic acrylics**, especially the ones that have bronze powder in them. These are really shimmery and they are especially nice for the last surface wash.

Embellishments

Embellishments really add to the look of the finished pieces, and almost anything can be used to make them. Here are a few ideas:

Clay embellishments

I make a lot of my own clay embellishments, and some special equipment is needed to make them.

I use a lot of **air-drying paper clay** and prefer the heavier weight type. That said, you can stitch through lightweight types, which is useful. Regardless of what weight you choose, a **small rolling pin** is used to make a flat, even surface in the clay.

Texture mats or **printing blocks** are used to impress patterns on to the clay and I use **cookie cutters** to cut out shapes. You can get tiny ones for sugarcraft, which are ideal.

For finishing your clay embellishments, and for general highlights, **metallic rub-on gilt wax** is particularly effective.

Other embellishments

I have a nice collection of differently-shaped and sized **paper punches**. They can be a bit expensive but I have found them very useful. You can punch **chocolate wrapper foil** as well as paper, so I get all my friends and family eating sweets so I can get as many coloured foils as possible! They can be attached using fusible web. **Beads**, **buttons** and **sequins** have proved useful as additions to punched paper shapes.

Cocktail sticks look nice couched down in rows. Ordinary **sale tags** are nice when you paint and stitch them, and by layering **paper shapes**, **sequins**, **craft jewels** and **beads** on them, you can make a stunning hanging embellishment for your artwork, book or whatever project you are doing.

There are many different **eyelets** on the market now. For the projects you will see in this book, I am using simple clothing eyelets.

I also use **heat-transfer foil**, which can be ironed on to any sticky surface, such as fusible web, plexi glue (which stays sticky when dry) or acrylic paint.

In later projects you will need little **brass hinges**, which can be purchased from any good hardware store. The little **candles** I use in the bookshrine (see page 75) are birthday cake candles with holders. I have used **jewellery findings** like earring hooks to dangle accents such as tags from holes in my work. There are a huge variety of **brads** on the market – these are split pins with a decorative head that can be pushed through your work to attach other things, such as paper flowers and hanging embellishments.

Tip

The best foils to use are metallic. If they tear easily, they are pure aluminium foil which is ideal. Wrappers covered in plastic are not as useful.

Other materials

There are a few other items that you will need for the projects in this book.

Children's washable PVA is used to treat the interlining and for general gluing, while **professional-quality crafter's PVA** is used for fixing heavy attachments in place where children's glue will not hold.

A **glue stick** is used for temporary attachment whilst stitching.

Fusible web is glue carried on a paper sheet that you can transfer by using an iron. It is useful for sticking tissues and fabrics and for attaching foils.

Cutting mat and **craft knife** I find the self-healing mats really good. Get a safety knife that you can retract, especially if you have children around. A **metal-edged ruler** is very useful and much safer than a plastic one. You can also tear papers against it, which gives a slightly rough edge.

A pair of **large scissors** and some **smaller sharp scissors** are used for cutting up paper and cloth, and for trimming threads.

A **hammer** is used to attach eyelet embellishments.

A **stiletto** is used for poking holes into the thicker fabrics.

An **emery board** is handy for tidying up the edges of dried clay embellishments.

An **iron** and **ironing pad** I have made an ironing pad out of a piece of chipboard covered with interlining and calico. **Silicone baking parchment** should always be used when ironing over sticky surfaces, because it protects the iron and helps to disperse the heat over the ironed area.

Gesso This is the primer used on artists' canvases, and you will be using it to seal your surfaces. Please use a good-quality one; cheap ones are really thin and do not seal well. You can use a matt household emulsion at a push but this can be a bit absorbent.

You will need some **paintbrushes**, some for painting and some for gluing. I like using household paintbrushes because their stiff bristles mean you can really get the gesso into all of the nooks and crannies. You will also need some **water pots** and a **palette**.

Finally, a pot of **strong black tea** will come in useful for staining cloth and paper.

Tip
An ironing pad is also brilliant for printing on, especially if you are using wooden blocks.

Techniques

Usually, when making an embroidered textile piece, you would colour your fabrics and stitch your surface with coloured threads, but with this mixed media method the surface is prepared and stitched before the colour is applied.

The basic mixed media technique that I use in my work begins with a background of stiffened interlining, a layer of texture, tissues, lace papers, fabrics and stitch. The whole surface is then painted with gesso to 'seal' the surface, then painted again with washes of acrylic paint. This technique takes advantage of watered-down acrylic paint's tendency to fall into the texture of the surface.

Preparing the surface

Stiffening the interlining

You will need to prepare the interlining before you begin a project. I usually prepare a large batch so that I have it ready for all sorts of uses, from boxes to book covers. You will need washable PVA and water to prepare the interlining.

1. Mix two litres of water (3½ pints) and two cupfuls of PVA glue together in a bucket.

2. Put the interlining in the bucket and soak it thoroughly in the PVA solution. Squeeze it out thoroughly, and repeat until it is saturated with the solution.

3. Hang the interlining out to dry overnight. Do not flatten it out, but allow it to dry wrinkled. This adds to the texture.

4. The stiffened interlining can now be rolled up for storage, or used straight away.

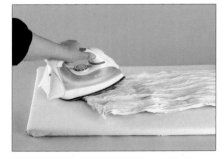

5. When you are ready to use it, iron the interlining flat. Use a hot iron with plenty of steam. You will not get all of the wrinkles out, but it will leave lovely wrinkled ridges.

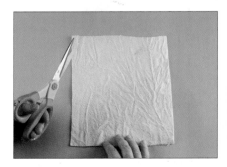

6. Cut the interlining to the size you need.

Layering tissue and fabric

Prepare the surface for stitch by adding textural materials such as scrunched-up tissue, scrim and lace. The more texture, the better – it will make an interesting surface for painting later.

1. Prepare a thin solution of PVA and water – roughly one tablespoon of PVA into half-a-cupful of water.

2. Tear the tissue paper into rough strips.

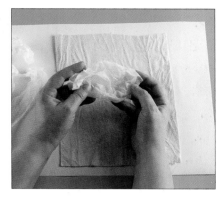

3. Screw up the strips to add texture and then open them out.

4. Wet the interlining with the PVA solution, then lay the strips of tissue on top and cover them with the PVA solution.

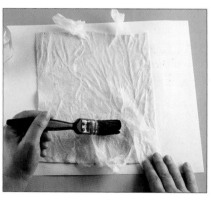

5. Continue laying the strips until the whole surface of the interlining has been covered.

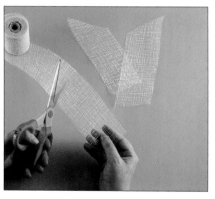

6. Cut some rough strips from the roll of scrim and cut halfway down into the strips of scrim, to split the ends into three or four parts.

7. Wet the interlining with the PVA solution and place the scrim on the interlining. Wet the whole piece with PVA to flatten the materials together.

8. While the piece is still wet, take the scrim strips and twist and pull them to suggest movement.

9. Repeat the cutting, wetting and placing process with the lace, and leave to dry overnight.

Straight stitch

Here you will be using machine straight stitch to suggest grasses blowing in the breeze. It will also serve to hold down any loose fabric or paper and it also marks out the general direction of stitch when you come to work from the back. You can jump from one line of stitch to the other without cutting the thread. When you have finished, snip them all. The loose threads will add to the textured surface of the finished piece.

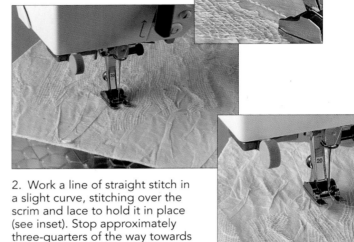

1. Wind the bobbin with ordinary white thread and set your sewing machine at normal tension at the top. Thread the machine and set it for straight stitch, then place the bottom of the prepared fabric in the machine and drop the foot.

2. Work a line of straight stitch in a slight curve, stitching over the scrim and lace to hold it in place (see inset). Stop approximately three-quarters of the way towards the top.

3. Make sure the needle is up, then lift the foot and move the fabric to begin working back down from another spot.

4. Drop the foot and work back down the fabric to the bottom.

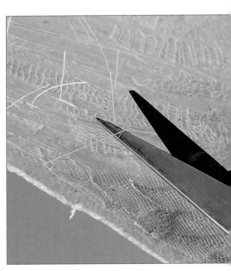

5. Repeat this all across the fabric, stitching lines to represent grasses, then remove the fabric from the machine and cut the thread.

6. Snip the threads that join the rows of machine stitch, and leave them free.

Cable stitch

This stitch will raise the surface texture slightly, and is worked from the back of the fabric with a heavier thread in the bobbin. I have used perlé cotton thread here, but you could try different ones to see which works best with your machine. If you do not have a bobbin case with your machine, do not despair! Most top-loading bobbins will work just as well, but do make sure to stick to perlé cotton thread when you begin, as it is easier to use than the more exotic threads.

1. Hand-wind the bobbin with perlé embroidery thread.

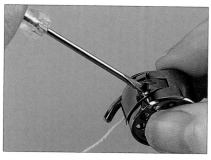

2. Thread the bobbin and loosen the tension slightly by adjusting the tension screw until the heavy thread pulls through easily.

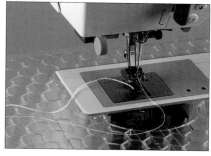

3. Set up the sewing machine at normal top tension and thread it with normal white thread at the top. Put the bobbin holder in the machine and draw the heavy thread through.

4. Place the fabric face down, with the top towards you. Note that you can see the back of the straight stitch. Stitch three-quarters of the way up, using the lines of straight stitch as a rough guide. Lift the foot, move the needle to another point and drop the foot.

5. Work back down to the bottom and repeat across the fabric, as you did with the straight stitch. When you have finished, remove it from the sewing machine, turn it face-up and cut the threads that join the lines of cable stitch.

Jump stitch

This textured stitch is an adaptation of the jump stitch that was used before the swing needle was widely available. The machine embroiderer, Dorothy Benson, was a particular specialist in this method on early Singer machines. The fabric had to be moved from side to side to create zig zag stitch (also called satin stitch). I have seen samples of her work that you would think had been stitched on a modern machine – faultless!

1. Set up the sewing machine at normal top and bottom tension and thread both the top and bottom with ordinary white thread. Pull the bottom thread through and drop the feed dogs.

2. Place the fabric face-up with the bottom towards you, and lower the foot.

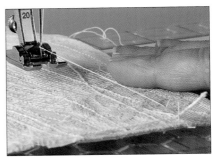

3. Work three or four stitches in one spot on the sheet, to anchor the thread, then lift the foot and move up the work.

4. Drop the foot and work three or four more stitches on the spot, then repeat back and forth across the whole of the fabric.

5. Remove the fabric from the sewing machine. This is the completed basic fabric.

Applying gesso

Applying gesso to the surface will now seal it, so that when you come to apply the watery acrylic, the paint will run about on the surface and fall into all of the nooks and crannies you have created.

1. Lay a sheet of scrap paper on your work surface and place the prepared basic fabric on top, face-up.

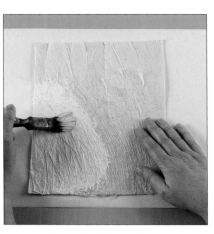

2. Use a household paintbrush to apply gesso to the fabric, working the gesso in and around the threads to seal them.

3. Continue working across the whole surface of the fabric. Use the tip of the brush to manipulate the cut threads so that they look like broken stems (see inset).

4. Continue until the whole surface is covered.

5. Allow the piece to dry overnight before continuing. It will dry more quickly if left near a radiator.

Applying paint

In this sample, applying the acrylic colour is the last thing to do. When I first started using this technique, I was nervous of colour and my pieces had a 'washed out' look about them.

   If you get the same result the first time you do it, do not be discouraged. You can always go over it again, adding layers of colour each time.

1. Squeeze some cadmium red, cadmium yellow and Prussian blue acrylic paint into the palette. Protect your surface with scrap paper and lay your dry gesso-primed fabric on it.

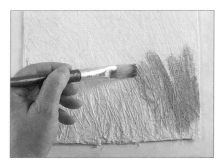

2. Use a large brush to re-wet the surface with clean water, then pick up a small amount of blue paint and begin painting the bottom right. If you put on too much colour, wet it with clean water and dab with kitchen paper until it is lifted out.

3. Draw the paint across the bottom half of the fabric, adding water to draw it out, and fade the colour towards the left.

4. Wash out the brush, pick up some yellow and add it to the bottom right, drawing it up in long brushstrokes into the top half of the fabric.

5. Continue adding yellow, drawing it across the blue and blending it with long brushstrokes to make rich greens to suggest long grasses.

6. Apply more blue to the bottom right to strengthen the colours there, and blend it into the colours on the fabric.

7. Add a little red in the bottom to further vary the colours, and blend it into the other colours.

8. Leave the fabric until all of the paint is completely dry.

9. Take some strong black tea, allow it to go cold, and use the paintbrush to wash it across the whole picture.

The finished piece shows how all of the techniques combine to produce a beautiful piece of fabric, full of texture and interest.

This detail shows the effect that is achieved by encouraging the paint to settle around the threads and textures on the fabric.

Machine stitching

Free machine embroidery can be a bit scary when you first start, but my advice is to keep practising. Try to find a place where you can leave your machine set up and ready to go, as you can sit down when you have a spare fifteen minutes and go for it!

Here are some stitches for you to try. I have used scraps of prepared interlining, but you can use stabilizer or pelmet interfacing if you can not get interlining. Because these fabrics are stiff, you will not need an embroidery ring: simply attach your free machine embroidery foot to the sewing machine, slide the material into place and begin.

I use a white cotton or polyester thread to stitch because it is easier to paint over white than coloured thread. You will need to drop your feed dogs (or apply the plate that covers your feed dogs if they do not drop down). Before changing your tension settings, have a practice 'doodling' on the fabric. Writing your name is a simple but challenging way to test your skill. The best way to gain control is to run your machine as fast as you can bear and to move the fabric slowly.

For some of these stitches, you will need to change the tension on your machine. This is easy on machines with bobbin cases as they have an easily accessible grub screw which you turn anticlockwise to loosen and clockwise to tighten your tension (get a second bobbin case for experimenting). If your machine has a drop-in bobbin, just change the top tension if you are nervous. There is a grub screw on the side of your bobbin case, but remember where the settings were before you begin.

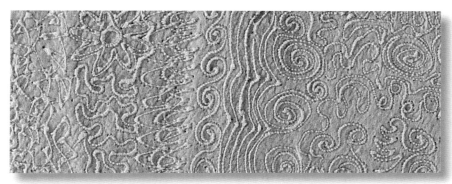

Corded whip stitch

I prepared my machine with the same thread in the top and bobbin, and stitched this sample in the vermicelli style, which is a wiggly freestyle stitch.

Tighten the top thread slightly and loosen your bobbin tension by a similar amount. Keep changing your tensions until you get good cording (i.e. the bottom thread pulls up to the surface, covering the top thread). Use the 'fast machine, slow hand' method of stitching for the best effects.

Feather stitch

This is what I call extreme whip stitch. It can distort the fabric due to the tight top tension but luckily for us, this simply adds texture. The top tension needs to be very tight to pull the bobbin thread right up to the surface in long loops, but the bobbin thread should be quite loose; again, you can experiment with this.

You will get the best effects by stitching curves and circular shapes. You can also try moving the fabric at different speeds under the needle so that you get different results. You can build up layers of stitch that look like barnacles with a little practice.

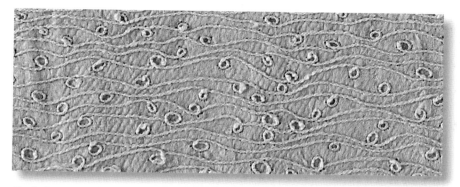

Cable stitch

You will need to hand-wind a bobbin with perlé cotton thread for this stitch, and your bobbin case tension will need to be loosened slightly to allow it to run easily. Make sure the top tension is normal, and begin stitching.

In this example I have drawn a wavy line with a little circle stitched now and then (think of it as a drunken wiggle!). In the workshops I run, perlé threads have run quite smoothly through drop-in bobbin machines. They do not seem to need a change of tension.

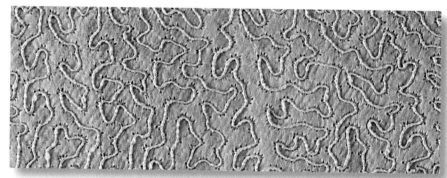

Freestyle vermicelli cable stitch

This stitch gives a subtle texture, and the sewing machine settings used are the same as cable stitch. I worked this example in a vermicelli style like the corded whip stitch opposite.

Straight cable stitch

Here you can experiment a little with loosening your top thread tension. Textile artist Alice Kettle often uses this effect in her work, as it gives striking big loops over her heavy threads. Run your stitches close together to get a rich texture.

Hand stitching

My forte is machine embroidery but sometimes I add a little hand stitching even though I am very slow at it. I use perlé cotton thread as it is easy to stitch with and shows up well when painted. The projects mainly use a simple lash stitch, but you could try French knots, fly stitch, or any others!

Lash stitch

This is a straight-line stitch I call lash stitch. This is a very simple stitch that I use to suggest plant stems or fencing in garden pieces.

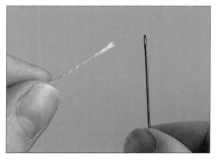

1. Hold the thread in one hand and the needle in the other, with the eye of the needle held up.

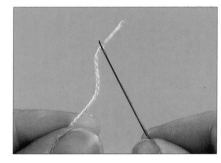

2. Slowly pass the thread through the eye of the needle.

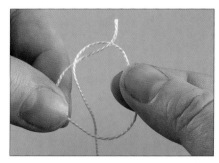

3. Loop the other end of the thread and pass the end through the loop.

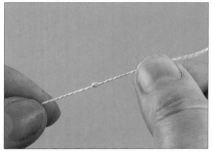

4. Tighten the loop to form a knot by pulling the thread gently.

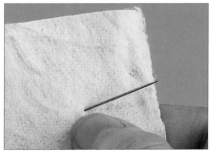

5. Take the needle through the fabric from the back to the front.

6. Pull the thread through and pass it down through the fabric, then up just below where the needle came up originally.

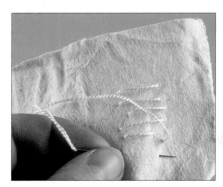

7. Pull the needle and thread through and repeat, working down the fabric.

8. Take the needle through to the back, turn the fabric over and make a few small stitches over each other to secure the thread.

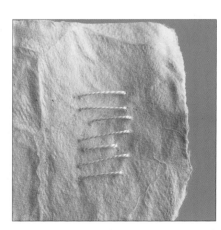

9. Cut the excess thread on the back to finish.

Meadow

This is a larger piece using the same techniques explained on pages 18–25. I have used tissue, lace, scrim and kitchen paper to texture the surface, along with straight-stitch embroidery. Heavier couched cords were also used, being secured in place with a zig zag stitch from the front.

Making your own embellishments

Making embellishments from paper clay

Paper clay is fairly resilient and quite weighty, even when dry, so it will hang well from the bottom of your work. The embellishments can also be stitched or glued to the surface of your work, making clay embellishments very versatile.

I often use textured rubber mats to give my clay embellishments some texture, and there are lots of different patterns available. Have a look in craft shops for your favourite designs. Cookie cutters are also useful for making clay embellishments, and can be bought from most kitchen or sugarcraft shops.

Tip

There are lots of different air-drying clays on the market. All can be used in the same way as paper clay.

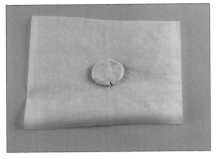

1. Lay a sheet of baking parchment on the work surface and place an egg-sized lump of air-drying paper clay in the centre.

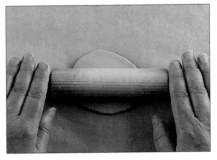

2. Roll out the clay with a rolling pin until it is about 5mm (¼in) thick.

3. Lay the texture mat on to the clay and press down on it firmly.

4. Carefully roll the mat off to reveal the textured clay.

5. Press the cookie cutter into the clay.

6. Peel away the excess clay carefully and set aside, then take away the cutter.

7. Press a mirror into the clay, and use a cocktail stick to make a hole at the top.

8. Leave the clay overnight to dry thoroughly.

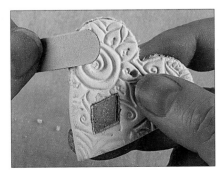

9. Use an emery board to smooth the rough edges of the clay. Check that the mirror is held firmly in place by the clay. You can secure it with a dab of PVA glue if it is loose.

Painting clay embellishments

I tend to seal the surface of my embellishments with gesso, but this is usually so that I can match them to the surface to which they are being applied. A layer of acrylic paint will also seal the surface, but experiment with the paint beforehand: the surface needs to be well sealed as clay can be quite fragile, especially if you roll the embellishments very thinly.

1. Paint the whole surface of the embellishment with gesso, including painting right over the mirror.

2. Once dry, use some watered-down acrylic paint to paint the surface, encouraging it to pool in the recesses.

3. Add a little pure water to the paint on the embellishment to enhance the effect and vary the tone further.

4. Allow the paint to dry, and use your finger to apply metallic rub-on gilt wax to the raised parts of the clay.

5. Use a pointed implement such as a stylus to scratch most of the paint off the mirror. Leave a little in place, as this adds to the feel of the piece.

The finished clay embellishment.

Making embellishments from paper

Preparing papers for use as embellishments is great fun once you get the hang of it. I have known students spend half the day doing it because they are having such a good time with the technique.

Make sure you use a good quality paper, 100–120gsm (80lb). I recommend painting both sides to ensure that, when you punch out the shapes, you do not need to spend time flipping them over to the coloured side.

There is a huge range of paper punches available in most craft shops, so have fun picking your favourites.

1. Put some cadmium yellow, Prussian blue, fluorescent pink and metallic green paint into a palette.

2. Lay a sheet of scrap paper down to protect the work surface, and place a sheet of good-quality printer paper on top. Use a large brush to paint the printer paper with cadmium yellow.

3. Allow the yellow to dry, and then paint over it with fluorescent pink. Add a little water to vary the tone and allow the yellow to show through. Allow to dry.

4. Water down some Prussian blue and paint it over the paper in the same way as the pink, allowing some of the other colours to show through.

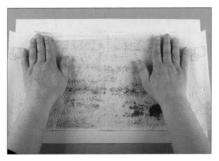

5. Before the blue paint dries, lay some textured or quilted kitchen paper on top of the paint and gently pat it to encourage it to absorb the paint.

6. Gently pull the kitchen paper away from the paper.

7. When the paper has been completely removed, you will be left with an attractive pattern on the paper. Allow the paint to dry thoroughly before continuing.

8. Paint some touches of metallic green on the left-hand side of the paper.

9. Add a little water to the green and rub it into the paper with crumpled kitchen paper. Continue adding touches of metallic green and rubbing it in.

10. Allow the paint to dry. This gives the paper a multi-tonal, lustrous sheen, and the metallic paint highlights the brushstrokes of the other colours.

11. Use a craft punch to punch out shapes.

All of these shapes come from the same piece of paper. Notice the variety of different hues and tones, but also how well they complement one another.

Star and Flowers Card

This card has both clay and paper embellishments. Notice that I have used a strip of paper with holes punched out as an embellishment – you are not restricted to using the punched shapes themselves.

33

Ideas and Inspiration

Experiment with different textural materials and make a sampler like the examples shown on these pages. These could be pieces that you practise the techniques out on before embarking on the projects.

Start off by laying down strips of various fabrics and papers, leaves, dried flowers and even feathers; then secure them in place with hand stitching and try some of your machine stitch programmes.

These pieces were made as experiments or demonstrations during workshops, but I like them so much that I have them hanging on the wall in my studio.

Tip
Leave flat paper areas so that you can add your embellishments later.

Tip

Make repeat patterns with card
or interlining. These experiments
could be quite formal in design,
or as loose as you like.

Tip

Iron on heat-transferable
foil to see what happens!

Tip

You could use white punched paper shapes glued
or stitched to the surface before the gesso stage.
Using rub-on gilt wax or pearlised powders over
the surface gives a lovely effect.

A Small Market Town

I have used the architecture of my home town, Ledbury in Herefordshire, to inspire this piece. A large clock tower dominates the town centre along with a half-timbered market house. The patterns and shapes of the buildings were distorted, enlarged and reduced, and I used the shapes to make the design for this piece.

A surface made up of collaged papers and fabrics applied to two layers of untreated interlining, gave the work a quilted quality when it was stitched. The surface was originally treated in the usual way, with gesso and acrylic, but I was unhappy with the colour. I left it for months trying to decide what to do, and in the end I gave it a wash of Prussian blue, which made a huge difference. I applied gold acrylics at the end which gave it an attractive, waxy look. The piece went from an ignored experiment to a framed piece I hang on the wall at home – I love it so much.

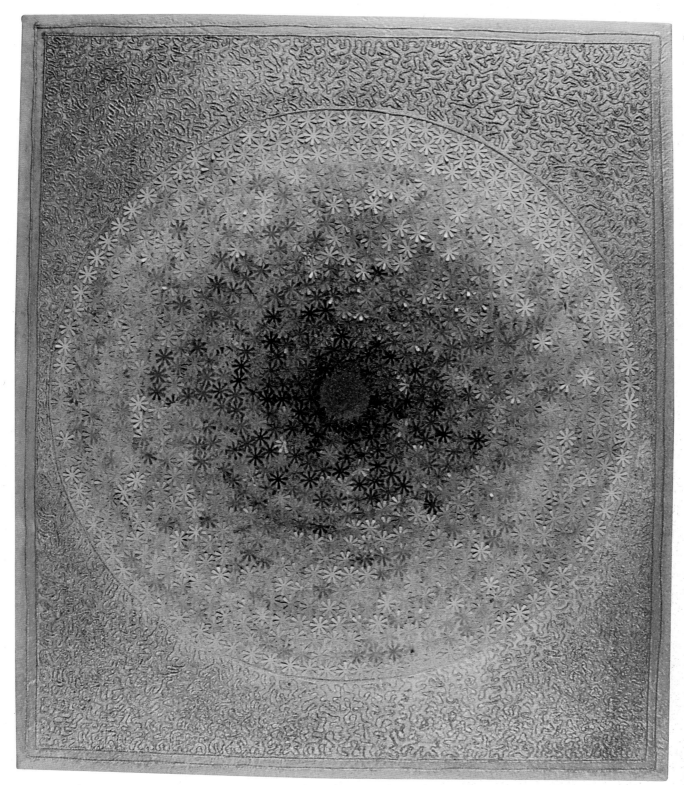

My Blue Place

This piece was made after a particularly busy and stressful time. I mark my diary in blue when I have time to make my own work and these periods are a lovely time for me. For this piece, I covered the surface with tissue and corded whip stitch in the vermicelli style (I love doing this stitch, I find the repetitive movement very relaxing). I used a metallic acrylic over the surface so that the surface shimmers and I find the grading of colour in the flowers very pleasing. It is quite hypnotic to look at.

Sunflower Bookwrap

This project was inspired by some old college notes I found in my files on making creative book folds and closure techniques. I had some lovely orange handmade paper that I wanted to make into book pages. In my paper punch collection I had some sunflower shapes and an idea for a bookwrap began to formulate.

This little A5-sized booklet is made using the basic method shown in the techniques section but now you get to try out your paper punches and air-drying clay embellishments. You will also learn how to insert basic eyelets. I think it is a nice, easy project to start learning the basic mixed media techniques.

The template for the bookwrap is on page 95.

You will need

Prepared interlining, approximately 45 x 25cm (17¾ x 9¾in)

Iron-on interfacing, approximately 45 x 25cm (17¾ x 9¾in)

Green silk, approximately 45 x 25cm (17¾ x 9¾in)

Nine sheets of Indian cotton rag handmade paper

Dressmaker's tissue

Fusible web

Baking parchment

Scrim

Sewing machine

Needle and pins

White perlé cotton thread

Cotton embroidery threads: white, stranded dark green and stranded gold

String and bobbly wool

Acrylic paint: cadmium yellow, Prussian blue, burnt sienna, metallic blue, fluorescent orange, burnt umber and metallic pink-gold

Large brush and size 2 brush

Hole punch

Gold heat-transferable foil

Iron and ironing pad or ironing board

Strong PVA glue

Kitchen paper

Printer paper and scrap paper

Craft punches: large sun, small sun and large circle

Eyelet tool, three eyelets and hammer

Thirty small gold sequins

Thirty small green beads and three larger beads

Air-drying paper clay for embellishments

Gold aluminium chocolate wrappers

Pencil

Scissors

Craft knife, cutting mat and metal-edged ruler

Gesso

Metallic cord

1. Place the prepared interlining on an ironing pad, then place the iron-on interfacing in the middle of the prepared interlining. Use a medium-hot iron to bond the two.

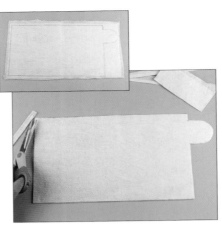

2. Use the pencil to draw around the template (see page 95 for the template) as shown in the inset. Cut around the pencil line with the scissors to leave the base of the book cover. Put it to one side.

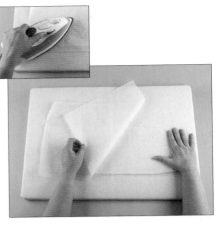

3. Place the fusible web on the ironing pad with the glue side (rough side) facing up. Lay strips of scrim on top, and a sheet of baking parchment on top of that. Iron with a medium-hot heat to glue the scrim to the fusible web (see inset), then peel off the baking parchment.

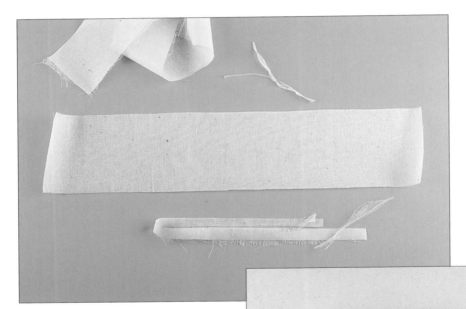

4. Draw a rectangle 45 x 9.5cm (17¾ x 3¾in) on the back of the fusible web, then use the scissors to cut along the lines, leaving a rectangle of material. This will become the top strip of the book cover.

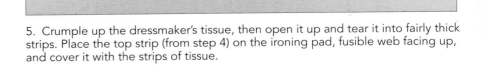

5. Crumple up the dressmaker's tissue, then open it up and tear it into fairly thick strips. Place the top strip (from step 4) on the ironing pad, fusible web facing up, and cover it with the strips of tissue.

6. Lay baking parchment on top of the tissue and iron it to seal the tissue to the fusible web. Remove the parchment and tear off any loose bits of tissue.

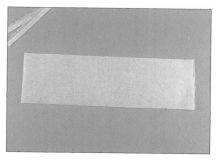

7. Draw a 38 x 13cm (15 x 5in) rectangle on the fusible web backing, and cut it out. This will become the bottom part of the book cover.

8. Peel the backing paper from the fusible web of both the top and bottom parts of the book cover.

9. Place the base of the book cover on the ironing pad, interfacing side down. Place the top and bottom parts of the book cover on the base, fusible web sides down.

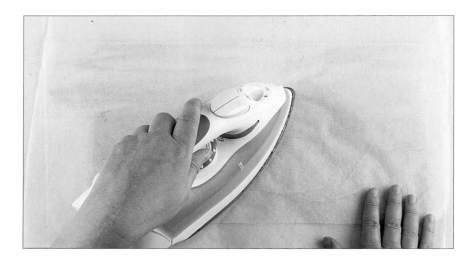

10. Cover the whole surface of the book cover with baking parchment to protect it, then iron it with a medium-hot iron to fix the top and bottom parts to the base.

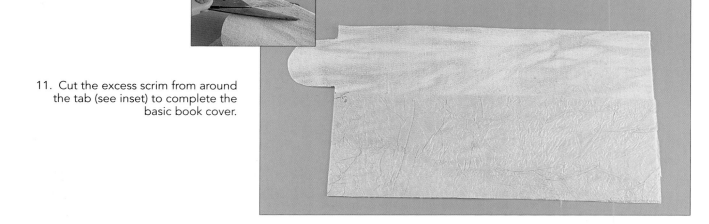

11. Cut the excess scrim from around the tab (see inset) to complete the basic book cover.

12. Set up the sewing machine by threading the top and bottom with white cotton thread at normal tensions. Place the basic book cover in the machine, face-up, and run a length of string down the join between the scrim and the tissue. Drop the foot and set your machine to zig zag stitch.

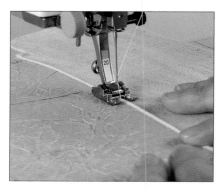

13. Couch the string to the basic book cover, using your index fingers to guide the string straight along the join.

14. When you reach the end, lift the foot and cut both threads and the string.

15. Couch five lengths of string along the bottom of the book cover in the same way, then trim the excess thread from the ends.

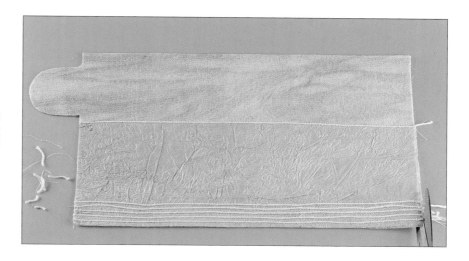

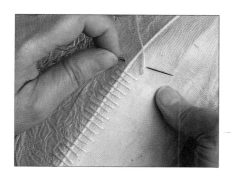

16. Work lash stitch in white perlé cotton thread along the couched string where the sections join. These are to suggest the stems of sunflowers.

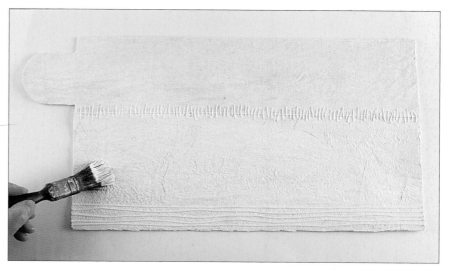

17. Continue working to the end and secure the thread before cutting it off. Lay down a sheet of scrap paper to protect the work surface, and paint the basic book cover with gesso. Allow to dry thoroughly.

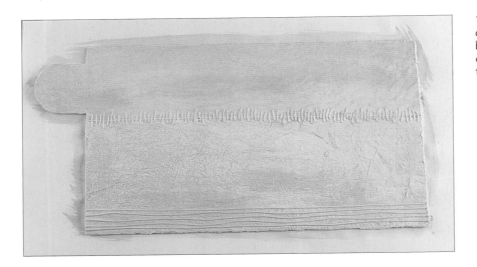

18. Wet the surface of the book cover with clean water. Use the large brush to paint it with watered-down cadmium yellow, working it into the texture of the cover. Allow to dry.

19. Wet the top part of the cover, then use a very thin wash of Prussian blue to colour down to the couched string.

20. Wet the bottom part of the cover and add a stronger wash of Prussian blue. Allow to dry.

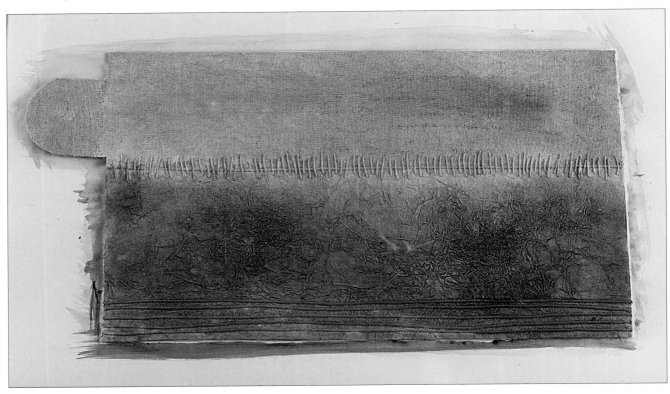

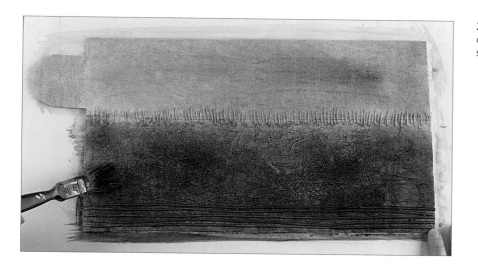

21. Wet the whole surface of the cover and apply a thin wash of burnt sienna to the bottom part only.

22. Use clean water to draw the wet burnt sienna wash up into the top part of the cover.

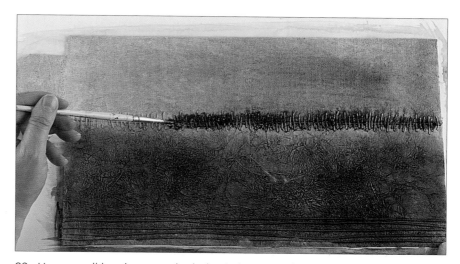

23. Use a small brush to wet the lash stitch area and apply Prussian blue along the join.

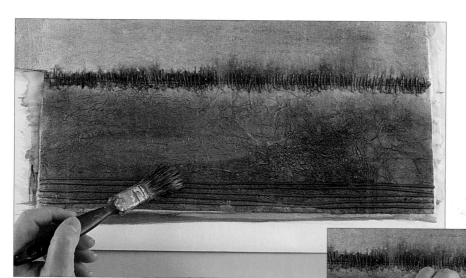

24. Allow all of the paint to dry, then re-wet the bottom part of the cover and run some metallic blue across the area. Use clean kitchen paper to dab and lift out some of the metallic blue paint (see inset).

25. Work along the whole area and leave to dry. Notice how the pigment has been lifted out, leaving the heavier metallic filings of the paint.

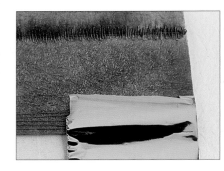

26. Lay the cover face up on the ironing pad and lay some gold heat transferable foil over the couched strings at the bottom.

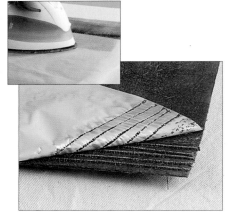

27. Lay some baking parchment over the heat-transferable foil, and use the nose of the hot iron to transfer the gold to the couched string (see inset). Wait for the area to cool down, then gently peel the foil off the couched string.

28. Repeat the process along the couched strings at the bottom, and along the lash stitch at the top.

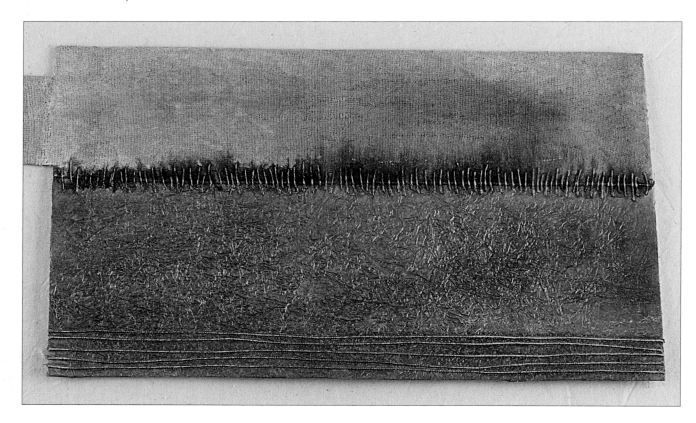

29. Put the cover safely to one side, protect the work surface with scrap paper and paint a sheet of printer paper with fluorescent orange acrylic paint. Allow to dry, and then overpaint with a wash of thinned-down cadmium yellow.

30. Allow to dry once more and overpaint with a patchy, uneven wash of thinned-down burnt umber all over the paper.

31. Once dry, paint a stronger wash of burnt umber on the right-hand side of the paper. Allow it to dry, then paint metallic pink-gold all over the paper.

32. Use kitchen paper to rub in and lift out some of the paint.

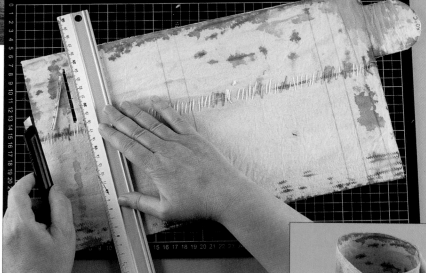

33. Put the cover face-down on the cutting mat. Cut a 60 x 2mm (2¼ x ¹⁄₁₆in) slot in the top left for the tab using the craft knife and metal-edged ruler. Refer to the template for the positioning of the slot. Roll the cover up to check that the tab fits snugly into the slot (see inset).

Tip
If you use up the entire outer edge of the painted paper, simply cut a strip away and carry on.

34. Use the large sun punch to punch a dozen suns from the painted paper.

35. Use the small sun punch to punch out twenty suns from the painted paper.

36. Lay out the punched suns on the book cover above the lash stitches. Rearrange them until you are happy with the design.

37. One by one, pick up the punched suns with your finger, apply strong PVA glue to the back and fix them in place on the cover.

38. Continue gluing the suns in place, then press them down with your finger until all of them are fixed securely. Allow to dry thoroughly.

39. Thread a needle with dark green stranded embroidery thread, tie a knot in the end and then bring it up through the centre of the left-most sun.

40. Place a sequin on to the needle and run it down the thread to sit on the sun.

41. Run a small bead down the thread, then put the needle in the hole of the sequin (see inset). Pull the needle through to the back to secure the sun in place.

42. Repeat the process of securing the suns with sequins and beads, working each sun in turn from the left to the right.

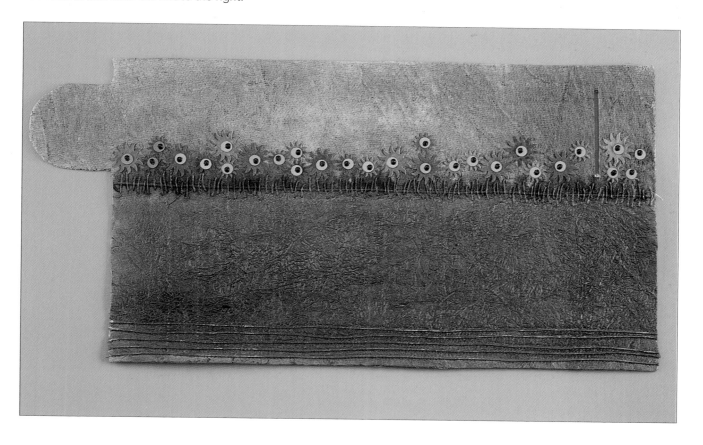

43. Cut out enough silk to completely surround the book cover, and secure the cover to the silk with pins.

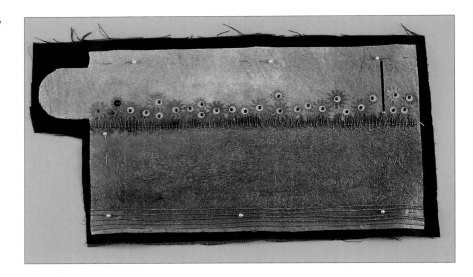

44. Set up the sewing machine with gold thread at normal tension for both the top and the bottom. Place the cover in, face-up, and lower the foot very close to the edge of the cover as shown.

45. Set the machine to straight stitch and work carefully around the edge of the cover. When you reach the tab, work round to the middle of the tab, then work into the centre as shown.

46. Turn the work, stitch a stitch or two perpendicular to the thread, then turn and work back to the edge.

47. Work around the rest of the edge of the cover, then carefully work around the edges of the slot.

48. Remove the cover from the machine and take out the pins. Paint some watered-down PVA along the stitches, to stop the silk from fraying. Allow to dry.

49. Trim off the silk around the edge with the scissors. Cut as close as possible to the stitching.

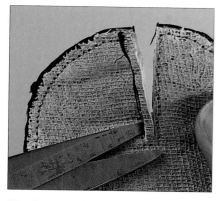

50. Cut into the tab to make a slot in the tab. Be careful sure not to cut into the stitching.

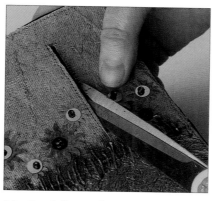

51. Carefully cut the silk out from behind the slot on the right of the book cover.

Tip

Test fit the tab into the slot once you have completed this step, to make sure that it still fits. If not, carefully trim the silk back further.

52. Set up the sewing machine with gold thread at the top and the bottom, both at normal tension. Drop the foot on the slot.

53. Set the sewing machine to a shortened zig zag stitch, and work around the slot carefully.

54. Starting at the edge of the tab, hold the metallic cord against the edge, and stitch very slowly: allow the needle to pass into the book cover...

55. ...and then down to the side of the cord. This will couch the cord against the very edge of the book cover. Work slowly and carefully so that the cord is well-secured.

56. Work all of the way around the cover back to the tab opening.

Tip

When working around the cover, work over the original line of stitching for neatness.

57. Cut the cord, and then work tight zig zag stitch in the tab opening. Cut the thread and remove the book cover from the sewing machine.

58. Make folds at the lines indicated on the template, so that the book cover folds up as shown.

59. Open the cover and measure in 3.5cm (1¼in) from each edge along the spine. Make a pencil mark, and the use the hole punch to make a hole at these points.

60. Use a hammer and an eyelet tool (inset) to add eyelets at these points. Work on the cutting mat to protect the work surface.

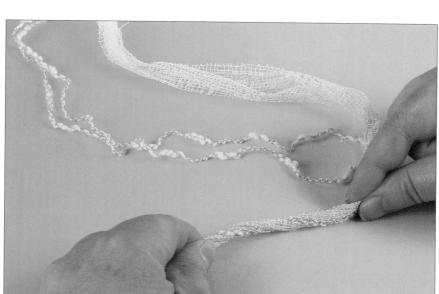

61. Twist lengths of bobbly wool and scrim together to form a cord. Set your sewing machine up at the widest zig zag stitch possible, with a freehand foot and gold thread at normal tension on top and bottom.

62. Drop the feed dogs, and then draw the cord back and forth to secure it. Remove the cord from the sewing machine, cut the threads and tie a knot in one end.

63. Tear the Indian cotton rag into roughly A4-sized sheets, slightly smaller than the cover. Fold them in half and then punch two holes in the fold, with the same distance between them as between the holes in the cover.

64. Repeat this on the other sheets of Indian cotton rag, then feed the cord through the holes and the holes in the cover.

65. Pull the cord tight and tie a knot to secure it. Tie a knot in the unknotted end, then trim any excess scrim and wool.

66. Close the book, feed the tab through the slot and put a pencil mark at the base of the tab.

67. Make a circular clay embellishment with a hole in the middle (see pages 30–31).

68. Punch a large sun from the painted paper and use the large circle punch to punch a circle from a gold chocolate wrapper.

69. Glue the circle to the embellishment using PVA glue, then stick the sun on top of the circle.

70. Thread a needle with dark green stranded embroidery thread, bring it up through the pencil mark and through the hole in the decorated embellishment.

71. Thread a sequin and a small bead on to the thread and take the thread back through the central hole. Tie securely at the back.

72. Wrap gold stranded embroidery thread around the embellishment, make a loop with the thread and take the end of the thread through the loop.

73. Pull the loop tight, wrap the thread around the embellishment three times, then feed the tab through the slot and under the embellishment.

74. Wrap the thread around the whole book two or three times, passing it under the embellishment, then wrap it around the embellishment and let it hang down.

You can add beads to the tassel to finish the bookwrap off.

Pink Flowers Bookwrap

This variation uses fluorescent pink acrylic paint as a base and paper flowers are applied before the first layer of gesso.

Green Garden Book

For this piece, I glued the collaged and stitched surface over two pieces of millboard before it was painted to make a proper hard book cover. I then painted it in the same way as in the original project. To finish it off, I added paper tags as a little feature.

Heart and Flowers Book Cover

This is a little bound book: I used the same techniques as the original project, but I stitched the pages together and glued them in to make a permanent sketchbook.

Indian Artefact

I found a postcard of an Indian miniature painting with a lovely man glancing at his lover. I thought I would like to use his image and frame him in an ornate Indian style frame. The design for this project comes from images of Indian architecture, particularly the layered arches and doorways.

I really wanted to use some fluorescent pink acrylic that I had. It can be a bit shocking to begin with, but you add lots of other coloured layers so it cools down in the end. You will learn about machine embroidery techniques, using bold colours, applying coloured tissue papers and T-shirt transfer paper. I love the colourful nature of this piece.

The template for the Indian Artefact is on page 94.

The design for the Indian Artefact. This is reproduced at three quarters of the actual size. You will need to photocopy it at 133 per cent for the correct size.

You will need

Pencil
Iron-on interfacing
Prepared interlining
Sewing machine
Scissors
Needles, including an
 embroidery needle
Iron and ironing pad or ironing board
Baking parchment
Cotton embroidery threads: white
 perlé, hot pink and stranded gold
Printer paper and scrap paper
Tissue paper
Fusible web
Scrim
Cotton
Gesso
Acrylic paint: cadmium yellow,
 metallic green, metallic indigo,
 metallic blue, metallic pink-gold,
 fluorescent pink, fluorescent
 orange, burnt umber, indigo,
 phthalo blue
Large brush and size 2 brush
Gold heat-transferable foil
Gold aluminium chocolate wrappers
Seventeen gold sequins
Thirty-one pink sequins
Forty-eight small green beads
Air-drying paper clay and mirror
 for embellishments
Craft punches: large sun and
 small sun
Stick-on craft jewels
Three heart-shaped gold brads
Gold cord
Iron-on T-shirt transfer paper
Thick card
Kitchen paper
Strong PVA glue and glue stick

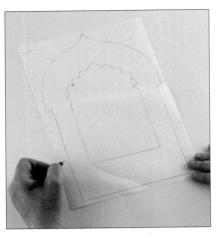

1. Use a pencil to transfer the template (see page 94) to the back of the iron-on interfacing, and trim it to size as shown.

2. Iron the interfacing to the interlining, then set up the sewing machine at normal tension with white cotton thread at the top and bottom. Sew a line of straight stitch (see page 20) over all of the pencil lines, then set the piece to one side.

3. Crumple up a sheet of tissue paper (see inset), then unfurl it and iron it to fusible web, protecting the iron by laying baking parchment over the tissue paper.

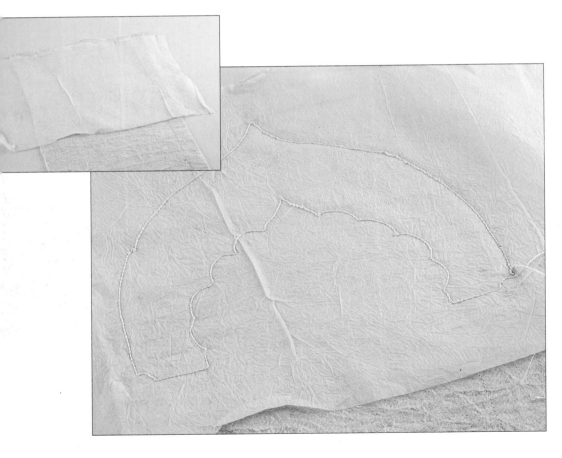

4. Peel off the fusible web backing and lay it over the top part of the front of the stitched interlining (see inset). Set up the sewing machine at normal tension with white perlé thread at the bottom and white cotton thread at the top. Place the stitched interlining in the sewing machine face-down. Drop the feed dogs but do not drop the foot. Sew cable stitch (see page 21) over the top part as shown, 2mm (1⁄16in) within the pencil lines.

5. Remove the piece from the machine, trim the threads and carefully tear away the excess bonded tissue paper. Iron the tissue paper, protecting the iron with baking parchment.

6. Iron fusible web to the scrim, then cut it into three strips: one 18 x 5cm (7 x 2in), and two 12 x 2.5cm (4¾ x 1in). Lay them on the front of the stitched interlining and iron them on. Working from the back, outline each piece with cable stitch as shown.

7. Cut seventeen squares of interlining, each approximately 1.5cm (½in) square, and seventeen slightly smaller cotton squares. Stick the interlining to the scrim with a glue stick, then glue a cotton square on top of the interlining.

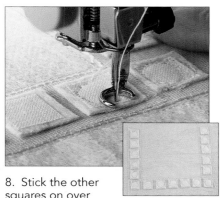

8. Stick the other squares on over the bottom as shown, then set up for free machine embroidery (i.e. normal tension, white cotton top and bottom, dogs down and foot up). Decorate the squares with circular motifs, repeating until all seventeen are decorated (see inset).

9. Adjust the tensions for corded whip stitch (see page 26) and work freestyle vermicelli over the top part of the stitched interlining from the front.

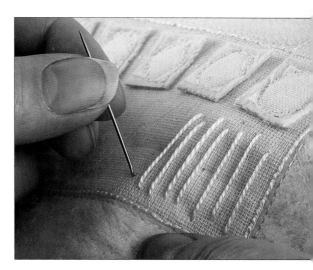

10. Thread an embroidery needle with white perlé thread and work rough lash stitch (see page 28) along the bottom of the stitched interlining below the embroidered squares.

11. Protect the work surface with scrap paper and use the large brush to cover the front of the stitched interlining with gesso. Allow to dry.

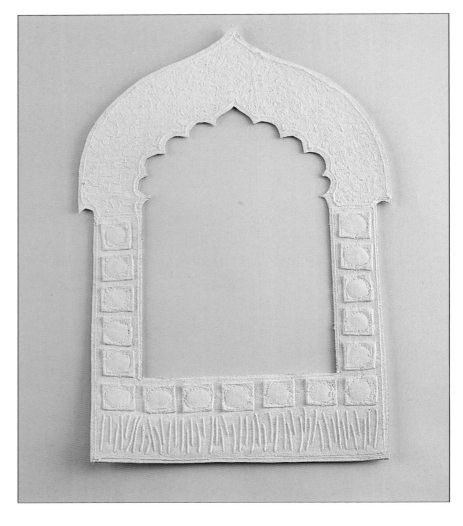

12. Cut out the shape with the scissors, just outside the original stitch lines.

13. Protect the work surface with scrap paper, then wet the surface of the piece and paint the top part with cadmium yellow paint.

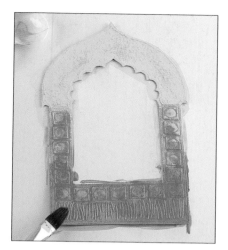

14. Working wet-into-wet, blend the cadmium yellow into fluorescent orange and then to fluorescent pink paint at the bottom. Allow to dry.

15. Wet the surface, then paint some metallic indigo paint over the piece. Allow to dry.

16. Cover the piece with watered-down metallic green paint (see inset), then leave for a few moments to allow the metallic flakes to settle. Dab the damp surface with kitchen paper to lift out excess paint, leaving a metallic shimmer. Leave to dry.

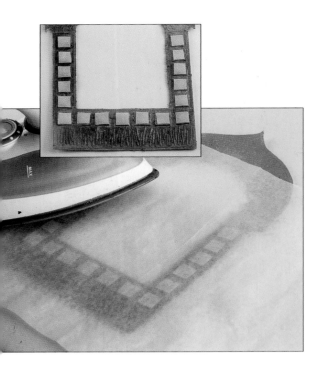

17. Place small squares of fusible web on the decorated squares (see inset), then place the piece on the ironing pad and use a medium-cool iron to secure them in place, protecting the iron with baking parchment.

18. Peel the backing from the squares, then lay gold heat-transferable foil over the left-hand side, colour-side up. With the tip of the iron, rub over the squares, using baking parchment to protect the iron.

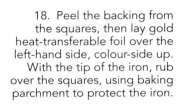

19. Carefully peel away the foil (see inset), then repeat on the other squares.

20. Prepare some painted papers (see steps 29–32 on page 47); the first with fluorescent orange, cadmium yellow, burnt umber and metallic pink-gold, and the second with indigo overlaid with metallic violet. Punch out seventeen suns from the first sheet and ten from the second, using the small sun punch. Use PVA glue to attach the purple suns on the squares, and glue fourteen orange suns to the top part as shown. Put the remaining suns to one side.

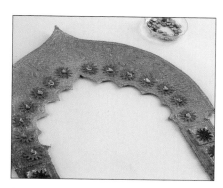

21. Use PVA glue to attach small craft jewels to the orange suns, then prepare seven teardrop-shaped clay embellishments and paint them with fluorescent orange, metallic blue and metallic pink-gold.

22. Prepare one more teardrop embellishment in the same way, but with a mirror embedded in it. Thread a needle with hot pink embroidery thread and bring it up through the left-most square at the bottom. Thread a clay embellishment, a large sequin, a smaller sequin and a small bead on to the needle.

23. Pull the thread through, then take the needle back down through the sequins and embellishment. Secure the thread on the back. This ensures that the bead will hold the other pieces in place.

67

24. Repeat the process across the squares, securing six other embellishments along the bottom part. Secure sequins and beads on the other squares as shown.

25. Turn the piece over and make an arch-shaped spacer from thick card, a little smaller than the piece itself. Secure it to the back using PVA glue.

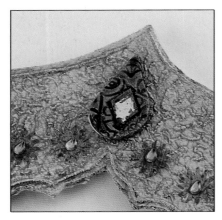

26. Secure the mirrored teardrop at the top with PVA glue to complete the frame.

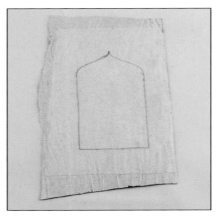

27. Transfer the inside of the aperture from the template to iron-on interfacing, and attach it to the back of a piece of prepared interlining with the iron.

28. Turn the piece over and paint the front with indigo acrylic paint. Allow to dry and then carefully cut out the aperture using sharp scissors.

29. Set up the sewing machine for zig zag stitch, with white thread at the bottom and gold metallic thread at the top, both at normal tensions. Make sure the feed dogs are up and the straight foot is on the machine. Place the aperture piece into the machine face-up and drop the foot at the top of the arch, clamping a length of gold cord in place as shown.

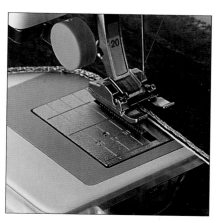

30. Couch the cord along the edge of the aperture, making sure the zig zag stitch is pinning the cord down on either side. When you reach the end, lift the foot and cut the threads and cord.

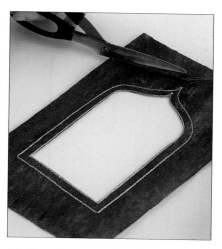

31. Couch a second cord around the first in the same way. Leave a gap of 1cm (½in) all the way round the inner cord as shown.

32. Use PVA to glue small pink craft jewels between the couched cords on the blue piece.

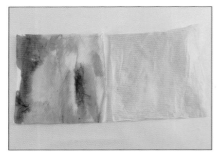

33. Water down phthalo blue and cadmium yellow until they are very dilute. Paint each colour on to sheets of tissue paper and allow to dry.

34. Cut a piece of interlining slightly larger than the aperture. Tear the tissue paper into strips and paste the strips to the interlining using watered-down PVA. Remember to protect the work surface with scrap paper. Allow the piece to dry, and then iron flat.

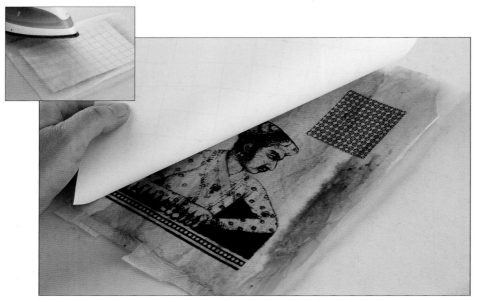

35. Transfer the design to T-shirt transfer paper and lay it face-down on the tissue. Cover it with parchment paper and iron it according to the instructions on the transfer paper pack (see inset). Allow to cool, then carefully peel the paper away to reveal the image.

36. Use a size 2 brush to paint gesso to the right of the figure, adding more towards the face and blending it to nothing further away.

37. Add more gesso to the top right of the face, then blend in metallic pink-gold acrylic around the top and left of the figure.

38. Use the large sun punch to punch three suns from gold chocolate wrappers.

39. Use a glue stick to secure a small sun from step 20 on top of each of the gold suns. Glue the assembled pieces to the artwork, just to the left of the figure.

40. Poke a hole through the centre of the suns with a thick needle (see inset), then push a heart-shaped brad through and secure. Repeat on the other two suns.

41. Set up the sewing machine for straight stitch free machine embroidery: dogs down, free machine embroidery foot on, gold thread at the top and white cotton thread at the bottom, with normal tension on both. Place the artwork face-up in the machine and drop the foot next to the bottom sun.

42. Stitch a loose square around the sun, then go over it twice more.

43. Stitch squares around the other two suns in the same way. Make sure you finish at the top right-hand corner of the top sun.

44. Run a wavy line up from the figure's head.

Tip

Feel free to experiment with free machine embroidery decoration rather than wavy lines.

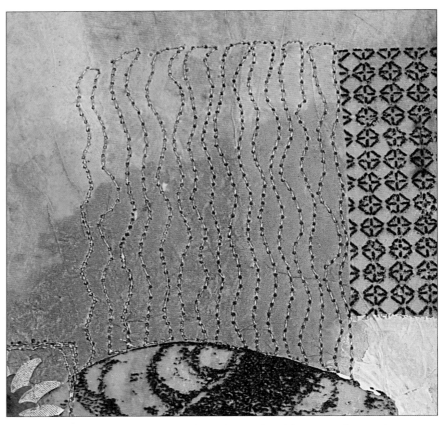

45. Work more wavy lines up and down the pink-gold area as shown, then cut the threads and remove the piece from the sewing machine.

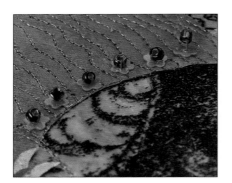

46. Thread an embroidery needle with hot pink cotton thread and attach pink sequins to the artwork, securing them with green beads in a row above the figure's head.

47. Add more sequins and beads over the pink area. Secure the thread on the back when you have finished.

48. Mount the blue piece on the artwork and secure it in place with PVA glue. Allow to dry, then glue the pink frame to the front of the blue piece. Trim away any excess parts, such as loose thread that show through, to complete the Indian Artefact.

Niched Glance

This piece is made from a frame from a boxed canvas. I simply cut away the material from the centre before I started. I added layers of foam board to make the recess deeper and covered the whole piece with layers of tissue paper glued on to merge the layers of board smoothly. The piece was then painted with gesso and coloured as in the project. The image is made in a similar way to the Indian man in the Indian Artefact project.

Indian Book Shrine

This piece was the first project I made when I was thinking about writing this book. It is made from an old book with a deep recess cut into it. Instead of using glued interlining as a base I cut a mountboard shape and prepared the collaged and stitched surface on calico. The surface was stretched and glued around the mountboard before the gesso stage. Other features include doors and a little shelf for the candles.

Sundial Diptych

I was researching diptyches for another project when I came across 17th-century portable sundials used by sailors. They are charming little things made from all sorts of materials such as metal, wood and ivory. I had a few small canvases in my storeroom and an idea began to form.

On the originals there are numbers and clock-face style patterns, and to suggest these I have use the flower circles. The 3D construction is a little challenging, so do not gallop too far ahead and make sure that you consider where the hinges and closures are going to go.

I love the way these pieces can be open or closed, and the gold cord is an intriguing element. You may not be able to get exactly the same size and shape canvases as I have, so get what you can and plan your design out on graph paper before starting.

A reference template for the diptych is on page 94.

You will need

Prepared interlining
Calico, 42 x 26cm (16½ x 10¼in).
Two small canvases
Pencil, ruler and compasses
Cotton embroidery thread: white perlé, hot pink
Large-eyed needle and embroidery needle
Fusible web
Tissue paper
Iron-on interfacing
Sewing machine
Scissors
Iron and ironing pad or ironing board
Baking parchment
Printer paper and scrap paper
Stapler
Strong PVA glue and glue stick
Scrim
Gesso
Kitchen paper
Acrylic paint: fluorescent pink, Prussian blue, metallic indigo, metallic green
Large brush
Transfer foil
Gold aluminium chocolate wrappers
Twenty-four small green beads
Twenty-four small pink sequins
Eyelet tool, eyelet and hammer
Air-drying paper clay for embellishments
Craft punch: small star
Craft knife and cutting mat
Gold cord
An image to place inside the piece
Two upholstery tacks
Two brass hinges, screws and screwdriver
Four large and two small wooden beads
Cocktail stick
Gold gilt wax

1. Iron the interfacing on to the calico and cut it into two pieces, each 21 x 26cm (8¼ x 10¼in).

2. Place a blank canvas on the interfacing side of the first piece and draw round it with the pencil.

3. Fold the edges up one by one and mark the depth with the pencil. Use the pencil and ruler to join up the marks, then repeat the process on the second piece.

Note

These measurements are based on the size of canvas I used. You should adapt the dimensions if your canvases are a different size.

4. Draw a 10cm (4in) diameter circle in the centre of one of the pieces using a pair of compasses. This will be the top of the sundial.

5. Set up the sewing machine for straight stitch (white cotton top and bottom, normal tensions and normal foot), then stitch along all of the pencil lines on both pieces.

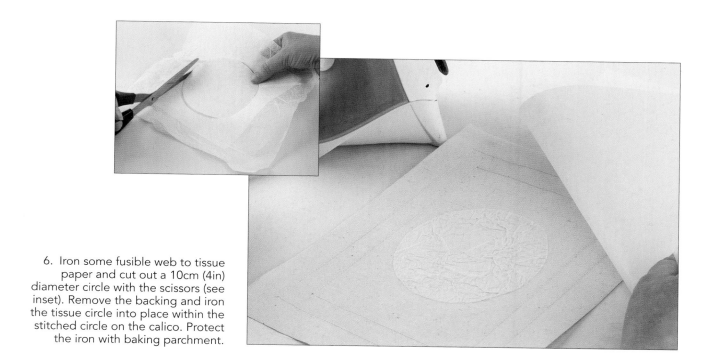

6. Iron some fusible web to tissue paper and cut out a 10cm (4in) diameter circle with the scissors (see inset). Remove the backing and iron the tissue circle into place within the stitched circle on the calico. Protect the iron with baking parchment.

7. Set up the sewing machine for cable stitch (white perlé thread at the bottom, white thread at the top, normal tensions) and place the piece face-down in the sewing machine. Stitch around the edge of the tissue circle, then stitch a small square in the centre, roughly 2.5cm (1in) on each side.

8. Work a cable stitch border, leaving 1cm (½in) from the inner pencil line. Remove the piece from the machine and trim the threads on the back.

9. Set up the sewing machine for corded whip stitch (free embroidery foot, white cotton at top and bottom, slightly looser tension at the bottom, slightly tighter on the top). Place the piece face-up and begin working corded whip stitch in a vermicelli fashion between the cable stitch border and circle.

10. Continue working carefully around the piece in corded whip stitch. Once the area is filled, remove the piece from the sewing machine and trim the threads on the back.

11. Cut out twenty-eight 1cm (½in) square pieces of plain white paper. Use PVA glue to attach them as shown, filling the long sides, leaving one short end clear and leaving a gap in the middle of the other short end.

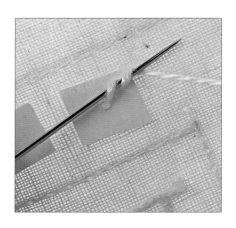

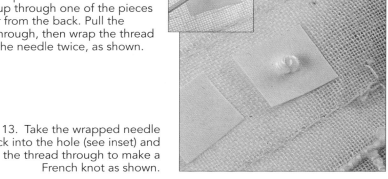

12. Thread the large-eyed needle with white perlé cotton thread and bring it up through one of the pieces of paper from the back. Pull the thread through, then wrap the thread around the needle twice, as shown.

13. Take the wrapped needle back into the hole (see inset) and pull the thread through to make a French knot as shown.

14. Stitch French knots into each of the paper squares, then add paper pieces to the other calico piece and stitch French knots on to it in the same way.

15. Place a canvas on the back of the vermicelli-decorated piece, fold the edge round and staple it in place.

16. Staple each edge in place, cutting the corners out (see inset) with a pair of scissors as necessary.

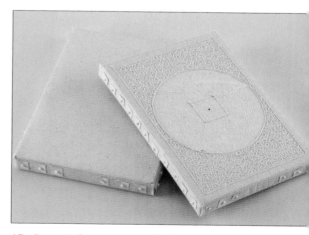

17. Repeat the process with the other canvas and set them aside. These will be the outer top and outer base.

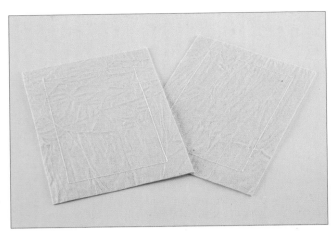

18. Cut two pieces of prepared interlining, each 15 x 21cm (6 x 8¼in). Iron on interfacing to the back. As before, draw round one of the completed canvases on to the interfacing side of each using the pencil.

19. Set up the sewing machine for cable stitch (as in step 7) and stitch a border 0.5cm (¼in) inside the pencil lines on both pieces. Remove the pieces and trim the threads.

20. Find the centre of one of the pieces, and use a pair of compasses to draw a 4cm (1½in) and an 8cm (3in) circle in the middle of the interfacing side of the piece.

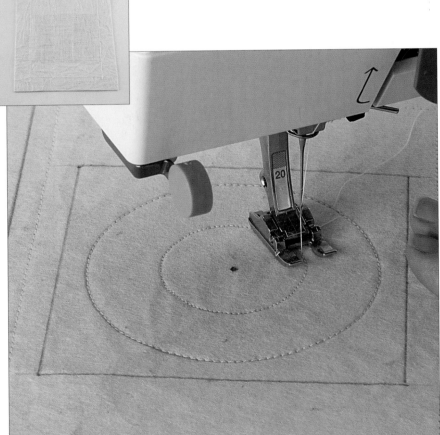

21. Draw a 10cm (4in) square around the circles with the pencil and ruler.

22. Turn the piece face-up and lightly attach small strips of scrim over the central area (see inset). Set the sewing machine up for cable stitch (see step 7), then place the piece face-down in the machine. Work cable stitch over both circles to secure the scrim.

23. Remove the piece from the machine, turn it face-up and carefully cut away the scrim from the inner circle and round the outer circle, leaving a ring of scrim between the cable stitch lines.

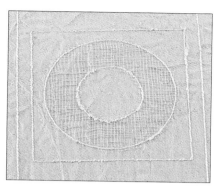

24. Work cable stitch around the square as you did for the circles.

25. Set up the sewing machine for corded whip stitch (see step 9), and work vermicelli (see page 26) between the square and ring. Remove from the machine and trim any loose threads.

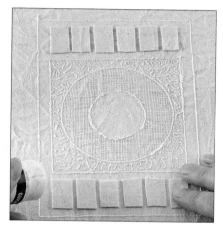

26. Cut twelve 1 x 2cm (½ x ¾in) rectangles from the interlining and glue them to the stitched piece as shown using a glue stick.

27. Thread the large-eyed needle with white perlé cotton thread and use lash stitch (see page 28) to secure the pieces of interlining in place. Once all of the pieces are secured, set the piece to one side. This will be the inner top.

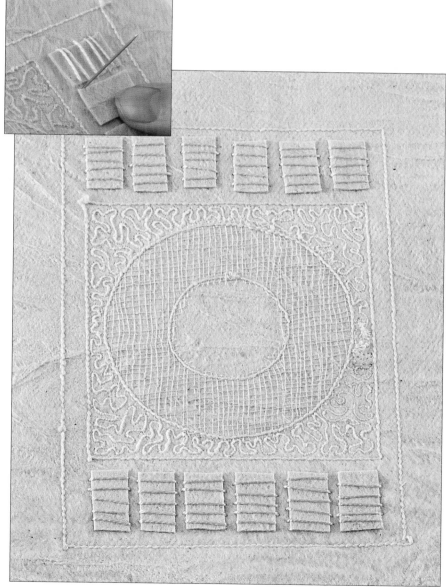

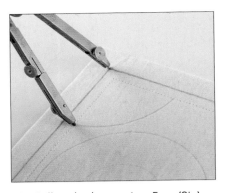

29. Still at the larger size, 5cm (2in) radius, put the point of the compasses on one corner of the pencil outline and draw an arc from one side of the cable stitch border to the other.

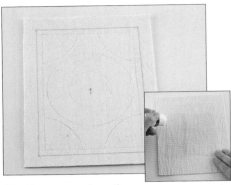

30. Repeat on the other corners, then turn the piece face-up and lightly attach scrim to the central circles with a glue stick (see inset).

28. Take the other piece of interlining, find the centre and draw a 5cm (2in) and a 10cm (4in) diameter circle as before, using the compasses.

31. Set up the sewing machine for cable stitch (see step 7). Place the piece in, face-down, and work the inner and outer circles.

32. Remove the interlining piece from the machine and carefully cut away the excess scrim, then replace the piece and work wedge shapes within the cable stitch border, using the arcs as one side of the wedges as shown.

33. Set up the sewing machine for corded whip stitch (see step 9), and work vermicelli as shown on the piece. Remove the piece from the machine and trim any excess threads.

34. Use compasses and scissors to cut a 9cm (3¾in) diameter circle out of interlining, then draw a 5cm (2in) diameter circle inside the larger one, and cut this out to form a hoop.

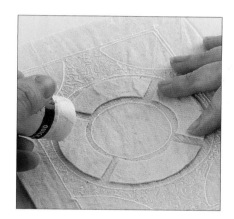

35. Cut the hoop into four equal parts, and glue them to the scrim area on the piece using the glue stick.

36. Set up the sewing machine for straight stitch (see step 5) and secure the pieces in place to complete the inner piece of the base.

37. Protect the work surface with scrap paper, then take the four completed pieces (inner and outer top and inner and outer base) and use the large brush to paint each with gesso. Allow them to dry thoroughly.

38. Take the outer top and paint it all over with watered-down fluorescent pink acrylic paint.

39. Allow the pink to dry, then paint over the piece with Prussian blue.

40. While the paint is wet, dab it with kitchen paper to lift out the excess and create patches of lighter colour.

41. Allow to dry, then paint the piece with metallic green acrylic paint. Allow it to soak in for a few moments, then dab the colour with kitchen paper to lift it off the raised parts.

42. Paint the other three pieces in the same way, then set them aside to dry.

43. Using fluorescent pink, metallic indigo and metallic green paints, prepare some painted paper (see pages 32–33). Once it is dry, punch out at least thirty stars with the small star craft punch.

44. Use PVA to glue the stars to the large circle on the outer top as shown.

45. Cut out a light-coloured piece of the painted paper and glue it inside the canvas using PVA. Put the piece to one side to dry.

46. Cut out twelve small squares from gold chocolate wrapper foil and glue a punched paper star to each using PVA. Glue all twelve to the inner top within the circle, as shown. Allow to dry.

47. Thread an embroidery needle with hot pink thread and bring it up through the middle of one of the stars. Run a sequin and bead down the needle to sit on the star.

48. Take the needle around the bead and back through the hole in the sequin and star decoration to secure them in place. Tighten the thread to secure, then embellish the other stars in the same way.

49. Use the scissors to cut carefully along the original pencil lines on the back of the inner top.

50. Carefully cut out the circle in the middle of the inner top, and use gold gilt wax to cover the white interlining edges this reveals.

51. Use the point of the scissors to make a small hole in the central square of the outer top (see inset), then use an eyelet-setting tool and hammer to set an eyelet in the hole.

52. Apply PVA glue to the back edges of the inner top and stick it to the outer top. Leave the piece to dry with a heavy object (such as a book) on top of it.

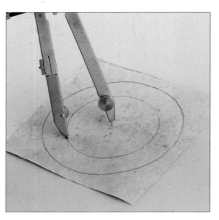

53. Iron some fusible web to the back of a gold chocolate wrapper and use a pair of compasses to draw a 4cm (2in) and a 3cm (1¾in) circle on the web side.

54. Cut the hoop into four parts, then fit them on the inner base as shown. Trim any excess to fit inside the hoop.

55. Remove the backing, cover the piece with baking parchment and iron the gold pieces into place.

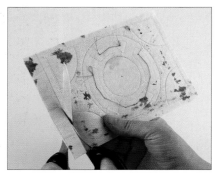

56. Punch out twelve stars from the painted paper and use PVA to attach three to each of the gold segments. Embellish the stars as before with hot pink thread, a sequin and a bead.

57. Turn the piece over and cut along the pencil lines with the scissors to trim it to size.

58. Use the craft knife and cutting mat to cut slits in the circle and wedges (see inset), then use the scissors to cut the slit areas out. Use gold gilt wax to decorate the white edges, as shown.

59. Thread the large-eyed needle with a 30cm (12in) length of gold cord. Tie a strong knot in the end and take the cord up through the inner base, just above the lower part of the hoop.

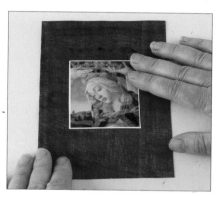

60. Make a 11.5 x 16.5cm (4½ x 6½in) piece of painted paper with fluorescent pink and a little metallic indigo paint, and use a glue stick to affix your photograph or picture.

61. Use PVA to glue the paper on the back of the outer base (see inset), then glue the inner base on top. Leave the base to dry with a heavy object on top of it.

62. Use PVA to glue a square of gold chocolate wrapper in each corner, then glue a trefoil clay embellishment on top of each.

63. Carefully apply gold heat-transferable foil to the sides and edges of the outer top, using a cool iron. If you are nervous about applying foil at this point, or you miss any areas, gold gilt wax can be used for a more subtle, complementary effect.

64. Work the edges of the inner top in the same way, then add heat-transferable foil to the base at the sides and inner edges.

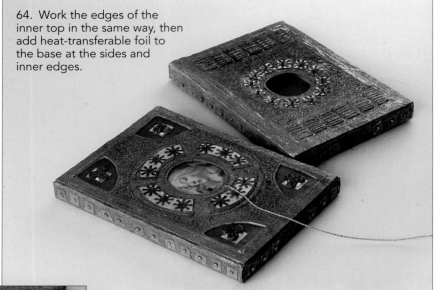

65. Mark the central points at the front edge of each piece, then use the hammer to knock an upholstery tack into each one (see inset).

Tip

For a more secure bond, you could use a hot glue gun to secure the beads on the base.

66. Place the top on the base and mark where the hinges need to go with the pencil (see inset), then use the screwdriver to fix the hinges in place.

67. Use strong PVA glue to secure a large bead to each corner of the bottom of the base and leave to dry thoroughly.

68. Glue two smaller beads to a cocktail stick to make a bar closure and allow to dry. Paint the closure with Prussian blue and metallic green and allow to dry. Trim the ends.

69. Thread the gold cord through the eyelet in the top.

70. Close the diptych and tie the closure on to the cord 20cm (8in) from the end. Trim the excess cord to complete the piece.

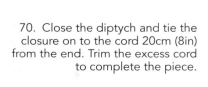

The finished diptych is as beautiful when closed as it is open.

Green Sundial Diptych

This was the first piece I made for this book. I used golden yellow as the base colour. This was followed by Prussian blue and then a blue metallic paint for the top layer.

Moon Sundial Diptych

The design was inspired by the lunar eclipse and the rain of shooting stars I saw in 2007. It is hinged with a heavily glued piece of hessian.

Templates

The templates on these pages are reproduced at half of their actual size. You will need to photocopy them at 200 per cent for the correct size.

The template for the Indian Artefact project on pages 60–73.

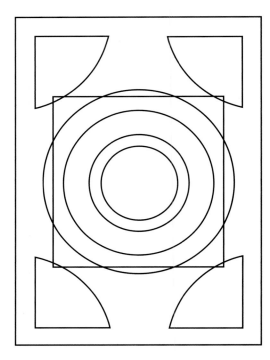

The template for the Sundial Diptych project on pages 76–91.

The template for the Sunflower Bookwrap project on pages 38–57.

Index